AN ARCTIC TUNDRA FOOD CHAIN

AN ARCTIC TUNDRA FOOD CHAIN

ODYSSEYS

A. D. TARBOX

CREATIVE EDUCATION•CREATIVE PAPERBACKS

Published by Creative Education and Creative Paperbacks
P.O. Box 227, Mankato, Minnesota 56002
Creative Education and Creative Paperbacks
are imprints of The Creative Company
www.thecreativecompany.us

Design and production by Blue Design
Art direction by Rita Marshall
Printed in the United States of America

Photographs by Alamy (Arco Images, Arctos Images, Robert
E. Barber, Blickwinkel, BRUCE COLEMAN INC., Bryan & Cherry
Alexander Photography, Papilio, Peter Arnold Inc, John
Schwieder, DAVID J SLATER, David Tipling, Visual & Written
SL, Jim Zuckerman), Getty Images (Altrendo Nature, Daniel J
Cox, Michael Durham, Jim & Jamie Dutcher, Andre Gallant, Ben
Hall, Johnny Johnson, Roine Magnusso, National Geographic,
Paul Nicklen, Patricio Robles Gil/Sierra Madre, Norbert Rosing,
Paul Souders, Gary Vestal)

Library of Congress Cataloging-in-Publication Data
Tarbox, A. D. (Angelique D.)
An Arctic tundra food chain / A. D. Tarbox.
p. cm. — (Odysseys in nature)
Summary: A look at a common food chain in the Arctic tundra,
introducing the Arctic willow that starts the chain, the wolf
that sits atop the chain, and various animals in between.
Includes bibliographical references and index.
ISBN 978-1-60818-538-2 (hardcover)
ISBN 978-1-62832-139-5 (pbk)
1. Tundra ecology—Juvenile literature. 2. Food chains
(Ecology)—Arctic regions—Juvenile literature. 3. Arctic
regions—Juvenile literature. I. Title.

QH541.5.T8T37 2015
577.5'86—dc23   2014038226

CCSS: RI.8.1, 2, 3, 4; RI.9-10.1, 2, 3, 4; RI.11-12.1, 2, 3, 4

First Edition HC 9 8 7 6 5 4 3 2 1
First Edition PBK 9 8 7 6 5 4 3 2 1

Cover: A polar bear
Page 2: An arctic fox
Pages 4–5: A snowy owl
Page 6: A Dall sheep

CONTENTS

Introduction

A bird swoops through the sky. In the depths of the sea, a whale dives. A wolf runs for miles across a snow-covered plain. They fly, swim, and travel in search of food. Animals spend most of their time looking for a plant or animal to eat, which will nourish them, provide energy, or help their offspring survive. A food chain shows what living things in an area eat. Plants, called producers, are the first link

OPPOSITE: This late-summer photo captures a classic tundra landscape—rocky terrain colored by lichen and short wildflowers, a shallow pool of open water, and a glacier.

on a food chain. Consumers, or animals that eat plants or other animals, make up the other links. The higher an animal is on the food chain, the less energy it receives from eating the animal below it. This is why there are more plants than plant eaters, and even fewer top consumers. Most animals eat more than one kind of plant or animal. Food webs show all of the possible food chains within a wildlife community.

The arctic tundra is a cold and dry **biome**. The dwarf plants that dot the landscape survive in this extreme environment because of their shallow roots and ability to grow quickly. Many animals have white, thick fur or feathers to match the ground that is so often covered in snow. Other animals have fur that blends with the colors of the summer terrain but later changes to match the snow. Despite the harshness of the land, 48 different **mammals** and a surprising number of birds and insects live here. And most of them do not hibernate; the winters are too long for that to be an option. Some of the animals **migrate** when food becomes scarce. Those who stay year-round live off the fat on their bodies to make it through the lean times. The plants and animals on the arctic tundra make up numerous food chains, including one that begins with a willow and ends with a wolf.

Arctic Willow: A Tundra Treasure

The arctic tundra, located at latitude 55 to 70° north, covers roughly 20 percent of Earth's land area. As Earth's coldest biome, there are only two seasons in the arctic: a very long winter and a very short summer. In the winter, it is not unusual for the temperature to be -90 °F (-67.8 °C), and in the summer, it might reach 37 to 54 °F (2.8 to 12.2 °C). With its dry climate, frozen ground, and precipitation totals of fewer than 15 inches (38.1 cm) a year, the arctic tundra has a lot in common with deserts.

Long ago, the Finnish named the place *tunturi*, which means "barren land." In the middle of the winter, when it is dark, with the wind blowing more than 60 miles (96.6 km) per hour and only blankets of white in all directions, the arctic tundra does indeed look like a barren land. Formed about 10,000 years ago, the arctic tundra is considered a young biome. Despite its youth, however, it bears many human imprints. Military testing, mining, and drilling have all left scars on the landscape. Tire tracks left on the snow were at first shallow impressions made by the weight of vehicles. However, these slight impressions have widened over time because of the freezing and thawing of the **permafrost**. Some of these impressions have widened so much that they are now as big as lakes in the summer.

In the summer, the arctic tundra looks like a very different place. The land comes to life with crawling and flying insects such as the hecla sulphur caterpillar and nose botfly. Millions of migrating birds return to wallow in the ponds created by the melting permafrost. Plants creep through the thawed ice and carpet the landscape with colors. This flurry of activity is short-lived, however. Within 12 weeks, the temperature drops, the insects die off, most of the birds leave, and the ground becomes white and frozen again.

Despite the harsh living conditions of this cold climate and the permafrost hindering the growth of trees, more than 1,700 **species** of plants grow on the arctic tundra. Most of the vegetation grows low to the ground

Lichen-Loving Reindeer

Weighing almost 600 pounds (272 kg) and standing taller than most men, caribou are sometimes called reindeer. Both males and females have antlers, although the female's antlers are not as large as the male's. There are about 5 million caribou, and they are an important food source for wolves, bears, and people. Wolverines also prey on them, and eagles and lynx hunt their calves. Migrating up to 400 miles (644 km), caribou may travel 50 miles (80.5 km) in a single day in search of lichen (which is often found on bare rocks because it has no roots) or vegetation such as grasses, tree shoots, or shrubs. Caribou usually start eating lichens in September, which is also the beginning of their breeding, or rut, season, when the males fight for mates. Striking each other with their long antlers and hooves, some males are killed or injured. After the fights, weary bulls are often killed by wolves, which bite down on their neck and nose and push them onto their side.

for warmth and protection from the wind. Plants such as the arctic willow are a very important food source for many tundra animals.

The arctic willow survives under the snow during the severe and constant cold of tundra winters. **Dormant** for about nine months, the willow waits for the summer sun to shine on its bark and melt away the top layers of permafrost. As if roused by an alarm clock, the willow wakes from its long winter's sleep. The plant's small leaves help it retain moisture and carry out **photosynthesis**,

even under a layer of snow. Its green, oval leaves are covered with woolly hairs, an **adaptation** the plant has made for warmth.

Spreading itself in low, reaching clumps, the arctic willow usually does not grow higher than eight inches (20.3 cm). Because the tundra's soil is always frozen, the willow's roots can penetrate only to a shallow depth after the top layer of permafrost thaws. The plant flowers in the summer but has tower-like, brown to pink spikes called catkins instead of petals. In the plant kingdom, plants are identified as male or female and sometimes can be both. The soil type and moisture available determine the number of male and female willows there might be in an area. Female willow catkins make seeds, and male catkins produce pollen. Flies that get male willow pollen on their legs and body often fly to female willows and

help the male and female arctic willows **pollinate** with each other. The female arctic willow is usually more abundant in wetter areas of the tundra, while the male is found in drier places. The arctic willow can usually live for 85 years, but the oldest ever discovered was 236 years old!

In some arctic areas, humans use the willow as fuel for fires because there is no wood available. The Yakuts, a native arctic people from Asia, use the willow for tea, and others use the plant's leaves or bark to make baskets and clothing. Many survival books list the plant as a possible food source in the event that a person is stranded on the arctic tundra.

For human consumption, the outer bark of the willow can be peeled back and the inside eaten without cooking. The shallow roots of the plant can also be dug up and eaten in the same way. Containing 10 times more vitamin C than an orange, the leaves of the willow are highly nutritious. For this reason, the arctic willow is useful not only to humans but also to a short, furry animal that can't seem to get enough of it.

Lemming: Suicidal Rodent?

Lemmings are rodents that have a plump, football-shaped body. They might not be heavyweights, but they are suited for life on the tundra. Their one-inch (2.5 cm) tail, tiny ears, and short legs are all adaptations that help them retain body heat. Thick, brown, waterproof fur also helps keep them warm. Lemmings use their long claws to burrow through the

Lemmings may find logs like this to shelter under in more southerly areas, but on the treeless tundra, they have to spend time and energy in digging out hiding places.

snow and make tunnels to their favorite **foraging** spots or to make their home. Even though they have fat bodies, if a hole is big enough for their head to fit inside, they can squeeze the rest of their body through the opening as well. Because snow acts as an **insulator**, lemmings make their nests out of grasses and willow twigs where the snow is deepest.

Male lemmings are usually larger than females and have a home range of up to 6.2 acres (2.5 ha). Females forage a much smaller area. Lemmings prefer to live near lowland areas beside ponds and lakes. There is more vegetation in these places, which provides the lemmings with cover from **predators** such as arctic foxes and skuas (large sea birds), grasses for their nest, and food. Lemmings do not store **caches** like some tundra animals do for eating later. Instead, they eat their food

Arctic Giant

The polar bear is as comfortable in the cold Arctic Sea as it is on land. Reaching 11 feet (3.4 m) tall when it stands upright and weighing up to 1,500 pounds (680 kg), a polar bear needs a lot of meat to stay healthy. A polar bear still-hunts for ringed seals and bearded seals on ice. The bear has an acute sense of smell and can detect a seal as far as 20 miles (32.2 km) away. A seal hunts for arctic cod in the cold sea, but as a mammal, it must come up periodically for air. As the unsuspecting seal comes to the surface to breathe, the polar bear's enormous jaws close down on its head. The bear then drags the seal onto the ice to feed. A ringed seal weighs about 120 pounds (54.4 kg) and can sustain a polar bear for a week. The polar bear is also known to prey on narwhales, young walrus, caribou, and arctic foxes. As it swims in search of seals resting on ice floes, the polar bear may itself be eaten by killer whales.

fresh; in the winter, they eat frozen plant matter to meet their energy needs. Only a quarter of the food lemmings eat is digestible, and because of their high **metabolism**, they have to eat constantly.

Lemmings usually live a solitary life and will defend their territories under the snow (or what they are able to dig in the shallow tundra soil in the summer) from other lemmings. Lemming burrows frequently overlap, and when two animals meet, they are not nice to one another. They bite, squeal, and even try to flip each other over, especially in the summer when it is mating season. Lemmings average seven babies a litter and have up to three litters during the short summer season. Females can breed again as soon as they give birth. The young are born with their eyes closed and are completely dependent upon their mother. After 11 days, their eyes open, and by 15 days, they can walk. Young lemmings are soon capable of breeding and sometimes mate as early as three weeks after they are born.

Lemmings usually do not live more than a year in the arctic, but some in captivity have lived as long as three years. They are famous for their population swings, and lemming **densities** fluctuate every few years because of the weather, predators, and the availability of plants for foraging. Usually about 80 lemmings can be found per acre (0.4 ha). However, during low population years, the same areas can sometimes be completely void of the furry creatures.

Lemmings have been seen dying by the hundreds. Some years, these normally solitary animals congregate near water as if attending a town meeting. The lemmings then enter the freezing water and within minutes are dead, their bodies eventually washing to the shore and forming piles on the beach. Lemmings have also been seen gathering on fjords, which are cliffs near oceans. Dropping from the sky like rocks, the lemmings plop one after the other into the churning waves, most dying instantly from the impact.

M ass lemming deaths were perhaps made most famous by the Walt Disney Company. In 1958, Disney made a documentary film called *White Wilderness*, which showed lemmings jumping off of cliffs. Most of the lemming scenes were fake, and the film was not even shot on the arctic tundra. But it brought

Clever Canine

Silent and sly, the arctic fox will follow polar bears for a bite of what the huge bears kill. With thick fur on its feet and covering its body, this 10-pound (4.5 kg) fox stalks its favorite prey, lemmings and tundra voles, under the snow. It also loves to sneak up on snowy owl nests and snatch young owls. The arctic fox digs through the tundra soil and stores its surplus food on the permafrost. During the short arctic summers, the fox takes on a mud color, which helps it blend in with the rocks and ground. When the snow returns, so does the fox's white coat. To keep warm, it burrows into the snow. The fox faces numerous threats on the harsh tundra. It may die from hunger or become part of the food chain of arctic wolves or polar bears. Humans also trap about 4,000 arctic foxes a year, mainly for their fur. Arctic fox fur is warmer than that of any other animal, including the polar bear.

attention to lemmings and spread what scientists today say is a myth. To most observers, these furry little beasts look as if they have committed suicide when they attempt to swim in freezing water or jump off rocks. However, scientists say that what looks like mass suicide is really mass **dispersal**. Lemmings have poor eyesight and simple minds. They are not trying to kill themselves but rather are risking their lives in search of food.

L emmings scurry through their tunnels and often pop out beside their favorite food, the arctic willow. Their teeth are sharp enough to chew and break apart even the willow's bark. As herbivores, lemmings forage for willows, sedges, and lichen night and day throughout the year. They do not sleep for extended hours like humans do but take short naps for rest, searching for food again every two to three hours. In the winter, when arctic willows and other vegetation are scarce and attempts at dispersal are unsuccessful, lemmings have been known to become cannibalistic, eating their own kind. When lemming populations suffer and are low, so are the numbers of many arctic predators. And when lemming populations are high, a long, tube-shaped hunter thrives.

Ermine: Curious Carnivore

Running across the frozen ground on its four short legs and often stopping to stand on two, the ermine behaves like a thief as it searches for a meal. With a body shaped like a foot-long (30.5 cm) hot dog, the ermine uses its sharp claws to dig dens and move snow while it hunts. Its tail is about five inches (12.7 cm) long, and the ermine is sometimes called the short-tailed weasel. Its fur is mud-brown in

OPPOSITE: Despite its small size and cuddly appearance, the ermine is a fearsome hunter. Its speed and aggression enable it to easily kill animals more than twice its size.

37

the summer and turns white in the winter, except the tip of its tail, which stays dark. The ermine also has another name: stoat. During medieval times, stoat meant "white fur," and it was common for people to wear the ermine's white winter coat as trim on their garments.

Ermines have a triangular head with whiskers, dark eyes and nose, and small, round ears. They are good swimmers but do their hunting on land or underground. Adults weigh only about a pound (0.05 kg). Because the ermine's body is long and narrow, it can squeeze through tight spaces, such as small openings between rocks. It moves with agility around corners and can run with good speed, ambushing its prey, such as tundra voles and young arctic hares, before it can get away.

On the tundra, ermines like to make their homes near lemmings. They live in the underground or rock dens of the animals they kill and can be found in grassy areas near lakes and ponds, which dot the tundra landscape in the summer. Ermines make their nest from tundra plants and line them with the skins and feathers of the small animals they eat.

Female ermines can reproduce when as young as two months of age, while males do not reach maturity until they are more than a year old. Ermines breed during the arctic summer, but the pregnancy is delayed until the following March. Females give birth to as many as 18 babies called kits. Males sometimes help with the rearing of the offspring, but usually the female does it alone. Kits are born naked, with sealed eyes. White fur soon fills in,

Fierce Fighter

It may look like a 40-pound (18.1 kg) bear, but the wolverine is actually a member of the weasel family. Roaming the tundra day or night, the wolverine does not hibernate but constantly searches for food inside its 1,000-square-mile (2,590 sq km) territory. It can swim well and is an expert climber, often ambushing its prey by leaping from a rock. With poor eyesight, it depends more on its senses of smell and hearing to find food. The wolverine is famously fierce and powerful, capable even of driving a bear away from its kill. Most of the wolverine's diet consists of carrion, or the rotting flesh of an animal that has been found dead. When the wolverine cannot find carrion, it has to hunt. It can kill animals much larger than itself, such as caribou. As a carrion eater, the wolverine consumes most of a dead animal, and the small remnants are broken down by decomposers such as tundra **slime molds**. Decomposition is very slow on the arctic tundra due to the cold temperatures. This is why the bodies of lost hikers have sometimes been found on the tundra years later, unchanged.

and around the third week, darker hairs appear. By two months of age, the kits are ready to start following their mother on hunting trips.

Ermines on the arctic tundra typically live only about a year, but some live as long as seven years. As carnivores, ermines are completely dependent on the small prey they can find to eat. When lemming populations are down, so are the numbers of ermines. Ermines are nocturnal and diurnal animals, which means they are active both night and day. Female ermines do most of their hunting in tunnels,

Ermines on the arctic tundra typically live only about a year, but some live as long as seven years.

preferring to live most of their lives under the snow. Males hunt above ground more, darting from rocks to shrubs in a zigzag course. They curiously stick their pointy noses in cracks and holes, often diving inside to investigate.

Male ermines may sometimes travel as far as seven miles (11.3 km) in search of prey, while females tend to stay near the place where they were born. Ermine home ranges usually cover about 20 acres (8.1 ha), and ermines mark their boundaries with urine, feces, and secretions from scent glands located near their rear. Both male and female ermines will defend their territory by wrestling and biting other ermines. Females are especially aggressive when protecting their young.

In the midst of the leaping, zigzagging movements typical of ermines, the animals pause to assess their surroundings.

With 33 sharp teeth and the stealth and speed of a cat, the ermine is a small animal's worst nightmare. Because an ermine has excellent senses of hearing, sight, and smell, it is able to locate even small and quiet prey animals such as lemmings underneath the snow or ground. An ermine usually detects a lemming by scent and follows the smell all the way to the lemming's den. Slinking like a snake, it then weaves itself through the lemming's burrows. When it spots the lemming, it moves in for the kill. The lemming's defense is to try to flee, but with lightning speed, the ermine attacks by biting the rodent's head and neck, striking over and over until the lemming is dead.

An ermine must eat daily to survive and will store caches of lemmings or other prey in its den. In this way, it prepares for leaner times, which occur often on the tundra. To start a cache, the ermine kills a lemming and bites off its head. The ermine stacks one dead lemming after another in a neat row against the wall of its den for a future meal. As it searches for lemmings to add to its cache, though, the ermine must always be wary, for flying over the arctic willows is a large, feathered foe looking to grab an ermine for dinner.

Ermines are skinnier than most tundra animals and therefore lose body heat more quickly. To help make up for this, ermines must eat—and therefore hunt—a lot.

Snowy Owl:
Silent Stalker

The snowy owl is the heaviest owl
in the world. The female is larger
than the male and can weigh more
than four pounds (1.8 kg). The white
coloring of its feathers, coupled
with its 27-inch (68.6 cm) length,
makes this large bird unmistakable.
A snowy owl has oval-shaped,
yellow eyes for diurnal hunting.
However, on the arctic tundra,
where it is dark most of the winter,

The feathers on a snowy owl's face guide sounds to its ears, giving it the ability to hear things humans cannot.

a snowy owl hunts mainly at night. With its **binocular vision**, it can see prey such as tundra voles from a great distance. The snowy owl has 3 eyelids that protect and keep its eyes from drying out as it soars through the air on wings that can measure 66 inches (168 cm) from tip to tip. A snowy owl cannot roll its eyes and must turn its neck—up to 270 degrees—to see objects.

A snowy owl's ears are not visible from the outside, but it has incredible hearing. The feathers on a snowy owl's face guide sounds to its ears, giving it the ability to hear things humans cannot. Each of its ears is a different size, and one is higher than the other. The differing size and location of each ear helps the owl distinguish between sounds. It can hear at the same time the distant hoofbeats of caribou, the flap of a willow ptarmigan's wings above it, and the digging of an ermine below it. After choosing which sound interests it most, the snowy owl moves its head like a large circular antenna to pick up the best reception.

S nowy owl feathers are different from those of most birds. The wing feathers have tiny slits like a comb, giving the owl the ability to fly silently. Reaching speeds of up to 50 miles (80.5 km) per hour, a snowy owl is a

To impress a female, a male snowy owl offers her a dead rodent such as an arctic ground squirrel. If she accepts, they become mates.

fast flier, but it relies more on its ability to fly silently than on speed. Feathers cover its entire body, including its feet, giving it warmth. At the edge of its tail is a gland that produces oil. In a behavior called preening, a snowy owl uses its talons and bill to spread the waterproof oil, which keeps its feathers dry.

Through a process called molting, a snowy owl loses and replaces feathers once a year starting in July. Under its feathers, the owl's bones are hollow, which gives it the ability to fly and to carry the extra weight of prey.

A snowy owl has a voice that sounds like a cackle, and it may hiss, snap its bill, and make a rattling noise when threatened. During the mating season, or when it is establishing a territory, the snowy owl's deep hoots can be heard as far as seven miles (11.3 km) away. To impress a female, a male snowy owl offers her a dead rodent such as an arctic ground squirrel. If she accepts, they become mates. A snowy owl male sometimes has two families at the same time, but the owls are usually **monogamous**.

Because there are no trees on the tundra, a snowy owl makes its nests on the ground, usually atop large

Hunting is more difficult for the snowy owl during the bright days of midsummer on the tundra, but its swift and silent attacks are deadly even in broad daylight.

OPPOSITE This male owl has returned to his nest and mate with a dead squirrel. The male will do most of the hunting while the female incubates the eggs and then protects the young.

rocks or hills. These raised areas offer the owl a good lookout point from which to spot predators or prey. In May or June, a female owl lays 5 to 15 eggs over several days. There is a featherless area on the female's body called the brood patch, which she uses to **incubate** the eggs. The male helps with the rearing of the young by hunting for the family.

The hunting range of a snowy owl might cover one square mile (2.6 sq km). Most of its prey is found by still-hunting, watching for potential prey such as snowshoe hares from high places. A snowy owl also ground hunts, walking on the snow and listening for prey such as lemmings or ermines. It jumps through the snow with its claws outstretched to snatch the ermine it has heard below. If an ermine is seen, the snowy owl does not take its eyes off of it. Rotating its sharply hooked talons so that one foot will strike the creature's neck and the other its back, the snowy owl swoops in for the attack with missile precision.

The snowy owl has one of the strongest grips of all birds of prey and can strike within an inch of its target, even at night. The ermine becomes paralyzed from the force of the impact. If the ermine is not instantly disabled by the blow, the owl uses its bill to break the ermine's neck. The ermine may then be flown back to the snowy owl's nest to feed its family. If the owl has killed the ermine for itself, it will swallow it whole. Even as it feasts, though, the snowy owl has to be wary. For there is another sharp-eared tundra animal that knows how to sniff out a bird.

Arctic Wolf: Tundra Top Dog

With 42 teeth and a bite strength of 1,500 pounds (680 kg) of pressure, the arctic wolf can crush solid bone as if it were chewing gum. Weighing almost as much as an average grown man, the arctic wolf is covered in white fur from its bushy tail to its black nose. Its dark eyes can detect even the slightest movement, but its keen senses of smell and excellent hearing are most useful in finding food.

OPPOSITE: Arctic wolves are closely linked with caribou. Wolf packs often move to follow caribou herds, meaning they drift north in the summer and south in the winter.

To other wolves, the scent markings read like a newspaper report, revealing if the wolf was male or female, whether it was sick, and how long ago it was there.

The arctic wolf can detect smells more than a mile (1.6 km) away and hear sounds up to 10 times that distance. Muscular and swift, an arctic wolf can reach speeds of up to 45 miles (72.4 km) per hour while chasing down prey such as musk oxen. The wolf trots so efficiently that it can cover 50 miles (80.5 km) a day. It is estimated that a typical wolf's home range covers 1,000 square miles (2,590 sq km), and it will hunt anything—from large caribou to small arctic hares—it finds within the territory.

The arctic wolf uses glands around its anus to spray scent, which is as unique as a human fingerprint, about every 100 yards (91.4 m) to mark its territory. Urine, feces, and ground-scratching are also used to mark territory. To other wolves, the scent markings read like a newspaper report, revealing if the wolf was male or female, whether it was sick, and how long ago it was there.

An arctic wolf usually lives as part of a pack that may range in size from 2 to 17 members. The pack has a clear hierarchy, and usually the smartest and most powerful male wolf, known as the alpha, is in charge. As the alpha, he chooses the female with which he will breed, and the two mate for life. Around April, the pregnant female finds a shelter, such as a pile of rocks or a cave, instead of trying to dig an underground den in the hard permafrost. She gives birth to four or five pups after a two-month pregnancy.

The wolf pups get milk from their mother during their first month but are then ready to eat solid food. When the pack returns from hunting, the pups lick the mouths of the grownups until one or more of the adult wolves bends over and vomits. This half-solid, half-liquid meal is the right texture for the young wolves' small mouths, and the hungry pups lap it up eagerly.

Wolf pups are vulnerable during their first summer. They stay close to grown members of the pack for protection from such predators as eagles, owls, and outsider wolves.

Each wolf in a pack has a job and a particular place in the pecking order. For example, a beta wolf is second in command, and the babysitter wolf stays behind and looks after the pups while the others go hunting. A wolf howls when it is playing and to get the attention of other wolves. It also growls and uses body language to show pleasure, anger, or apology. A dominant wolf will look directly in another animal's eyes if it feels threatened, sending the

TAKEAWAY

A dominant wolf will look directly in another animal's eyes if it feels threatened, sending the message that he or she is superior.

message that he or she is superior. A wolf of lower rank will lower its tail, hunker down, and keep its head lower than its leader's as it licks his face to show submissiveness.

The arctic wolf is a great survivalist and can go without food for two weeks. When it does kill an animal such as a musk oxen or Dall sheep, it is capable of eating as much as 20 pounds (9.1 kg) of meat at once. Because snowy owls make their nests on the ground, owls young and old are in constant danger of being detected by a wolf. An arctic wolf may first hear a snowy owl's young before it sees the nest. Once the scent has been picked up, the wolf follows it. If the snowy owl sees the wolf coming, it will almost always defend itself and its nest with its talons and beak. Hissing and screaming, the adult snowy owl makes a lot of noise, and, as a desperate final attempt, it may even act as if it is crippled to distract the wolf from its young. With one bite from the wolf's powerful jaws, a young or adult snowy owl's hollow bones and organs are crushed. Once a snowy owl has been killed, the wolf may pluck out some of the owl's feathers to get to the soft flesh underneath, eating almost everything but the owl's talons.

The snowy owl that the arctic wolf has eaten is linked to the ermine, the lemming, and the arctic willow in the food chain of the arctic tundra. One day, the arctic wolf will die from disease or perhaps be killed by a rival wolf pack. **Bacteria** will slowly decompose the wolf's body, returning nutrients to the soil. These **nutrients**, in turn, will allow plants such as the arctic willow to grow, enabling the arctic tundra food chain to begin anew.

BELOW Weighing up to 900 pounds (408 kg), musk oxen are some of the biggest—and shaggiest—tundra animals. They live farther north than any other hoofed animal.

AN ARCTIC TUNDRA FOOD CHAIN

On Thin Ice

Satellites in space show that the arctic ice has shrunk about nine percent every decade since 1978. Many scientists think **greenhouse gases** are causing global warming, and at this rate, they fear that there may be no summer ice in the arctic by 2100. When glaciers melt, the sea level rises, and scientists predict that by the end of this century, the ocean may rise more than three feet (91.4 cm), submerging low-lying islands and taking away land from every continent. Food chains and food webs would be altered because the rapid warming of the ocean and the land might endanger or even bring about the extinction of many animal and plant species. The polar bear depends on arctic floating ice to hunt, and scientists fear that the bear may become extinct if it cannot adapt. When people recycle and use energy-efficient appliances and light bulbs, solar and wind power, and even push mowers instead of gas mowers, they help to reduce the amount of greenhouse gases produced, which may slow global warming.

Selected Bibliography

Department of the Army. *The Illustrated Guide to Edible Wild Plants*. Guilford, Conn.: Lyons Press, 2003.

Hammerslough, Jane. *Owl Puke*. New York: Workman, 2004.

Johnsgard, Paul A. *North American Owls: Biology and a Natural History*. Washington, D.C.: Smithsonian Institution, 2002.

Mech, L. David. *The Arctic Wolf: Living with the Pack*. Stillwater, Minn.: Voyageur Press, 1988.

Wilson, Don E., and Sue Ruff, eds. *The Smithsonian Book of North American Mammals*. Washington, D.C.: Smithsonian Institution, 1999.

Woodward, Susan L. *Biomes of Earth: Terrestrial, Aquatic, and Human-dominated*. Westport, Conn.: Greenwood Press, 2003.

Glossary

adaptation   a change an animal species makes over time—such as growing thicker fur or eating other foods—to survive in its environment

bacteria   microscopic, single-celled organisms that can live in the soil or water or inside animals and plants; some bacteria are helpful to their host, but others are harmful

binocular vision   when both eyes of an animal, such as an owl, are used to see and detect the depth, height, and width of an object

biome   a region of the world that is differentiated from others by its predominant plant life and climate

caches   hidden places in which an animal keeps food to eat later

densities   the numbers of individual plants or animals in a given area

dispersal   the spreading or movement of organisms from one place to another

dormant   a state of reduced body activity in which an organism does not grow and its metabolism slows down

foraging   moving around in search of food

greenhouse gases gases that absorb the heat from the sun and warm the earth when released into the air; greenhouse gases can be natural (such as water vapor) or man-made (as from burning fossil fuels)

incubate to sit on eggs so that the warmth will help the young inside develop until they are ready to hatch

insulator a material (such as feathers, wool, or snow) that makes it hard for heat, cold, or light to pass through it

mammals backboned animals that have hair and nurse their young with milk

metabolism the chemical and physical process inside an organism that regulates the amount of energy used for activities and sustaining life

migrate to move from one climate or location to another to find food or to breed

monogamous having one mate for life

nutrients minerals, vitamins, and other substances that provide an organism with what it needs to live, grow, and flourish

permafrost a permanent layer of frozen soil found at Earth's polar regions; permafrost is sometimes as deep as 5,000 feet (1,524 m)

photosynthesis a process by which plants exposed to sunlight are able to make their own food

pollinate	to fertilize plants by transferring a powdery dust called pollen from one plant to another
predators	animals that live by killing for their food
slime molds	organisms found on dead matter; they are a kind of fungus with the look and consistency of moist clay
species	animals that have similar characteristics and are able to mate with each other

Index